The BLOSSOM DEARIE Songbook

Cover photo © 1983 by Roy Blakey

Special thanks to Jim DiGiovanni and Jaime Smith.

Additional thanks to Francis Birchett, David Rosner, Phyllis Buell, Anne Kaye, Mike Esslie,
Sharon Grace Powers, Karl Mansfield, Keith Mardak, and Mark Carlstein.

ISBN 978-1-61780-324-6

HAL•LEONARD®
CORPORATION
7777 W. BLUEMOUND RD. P.O. BOX 13819 MILWAUKEE, WI 53213

Visit Hal Leonard Online at
www.halleonard.com

BLOSSOM DEARIE

A careful economy rounded out the corners of Blossom Dearie's life. Off stage or on, speaking or singing, writing music or playing the piano, as a person or as a performer. You would see this self-developed economy in the ratio of piano to voice in her arrangements, in the pace of her concerts and in her recording output. You would also find it in the impeccable manner in which she spoke, in perfect rhythm for the situation, often in clipped answers. Especially when dealing with someone who tread into territory unwelcome with a question like, "What year were you born?"

Blossom Dearie was born in 1924 into what she called, "a very provincial existence." A happy family unit, her three older half-brothers heralded her arrival by filling the house with pear blossoms from a neighbor. Her father Henry Dearie was a hotel manager who was Scottish and Irish, and her mother Margrete was an immigrant from Oslo, Norway.

As a very young child, Blossom picked out tunes on the family piano with the aid of a natural ear and the lap of the nearest adult to sit on. At around two she was able to pick out Debussy's "Prelude to the Afternoon of a Faun." Piano lessons began at an early age with her teacher Miss Parks. Very particular about the music she wanted to play, Blossom often selected the pieces she wanted to learn as opposed to what her teachers gave her. At age 10 while staying in Washington, D.C. with her older brother James, she was enrolled in a course of study in classical music and was talented enough that it looked as if she would enter the Peabody Conservatory. Instead it was back to East Durham, NY, in the Catskills where, as she described it, "the wonderful music of the time" had a profound impact on her and she switched her piano studies to jazz. Musicians like Art Tatum, Jo Stafford, Duke Ellington and Glenn Miller gave her a sense of what she wanted to do with the piano. She was a hit with local and high school dance bands and often played at school functions.

After high school, Blossom ventured to New York City. Her brother Barney was in New Jersey becoming an airplane mechanic, and her mother came down initially to help her get started as a performer. Blossom took any job she could find and started hanging out with local musicians. This was the 1940s. She was at Birdland every night for three years taking in all she could with greats like Sarah Vaughan, Charlie Parker and Miles Davis. As a new performer, she started out playing the dingy clubs and took modeling jobs to make ends meet. Blossom credited Dave Lambert (of the vocal jazz trio Lambert, Hendricks and Ross) with introducing her to the world of vocals. She never worked with him but rehearsed with him and spent time as a singer with groups like Woody Herman's Blue Flames and Alvino Rey's Blue Reys. Hugh Shannon made an impression on her as he sang and accompanied himself on the piano at the Caprice on the East Side. This led to what she called the true start of her career. Performing special songs for a special, attentive audience appealed to her.

According to Blossom, it was 1950 in a small club in Greenwich Village called the Chantilly where she felt she truly became a professional performer. It was just a long bar with a piano at the back where she would sing and accompany herself on the piano. She would also accompany other singers who would show up: Tony Bennett would pop in, Annie Ross would drop by, and if they were there together they would do duets.

Blossom was struggling when she met Nicole and Eddy Barclay. They had a jazz record company in France, Barclay Records, and they suggested she go to France where appreciation for American Jazz was flourishing. While there she recorded an album for their record company. She also spent time at the Mars Club with performers like Bobby Short and Bob Dorough (accompanist for Sugar Ray Robinson) and Annie Ross. The vocal group The Blue Stars of France was organized by Blossom, who also provided the arrangements. They had a hit record with "Lullaby of Birdland" by George Shearing, sung in French, for which Michel Legrand did the arrangement. (Christiane Legrand, Michel's sister, was a member of The Blue Stars.) Visa issues prevented the group from coming to the States with Blossom, so she returned alone. The Blue Stars eventually became the Swingle Singers when Ward Swingle took it over.

After several years, Blossom returned to New York City and followed up on Norman Granz's offer, made to her in France, when he stopped in to hear Blossom performing at The Ringside in Paris. He suggested that when she returned to the United States she record an album for his Verve label. This led to Blossom's first American recording, *Blossom Dearie*. The coy jazz bird with the librarian's glasses that graced the cover of the album belied what lay in store for the listener: an acute sense of swing and bebop, and arrangements of well-known songs that had all their usual sentimentality and tricks stripped away. A messenger and her message.

What followed were five more recordings, her favorite being *My Gentleman Friend* which featured her husband, the Belgian flutist Bobby Jaspar. They had married in 1955. The others were *Give Him the Oo-La-La, Once Upon a*

Summertime, Blossom Dearie Sings Comden and Green and *Blossom Dearie Soubrette Sings Broadway Hit Songs*. She cared less for the *Soubrette* and *Comden and Green* albums because she had a cold while recording them and felt there was a lack in her piano playing.

In New York City Blossom was in the greatest of music circles, playing at Julius Monk's Upstairs at the Downstairs and hanging out with Steve Allen, Dave Garroway and Johnny Mercer, going to parties at Jean and Bob Bach's house in the Village. When she sang Michel Legrand's "La Valse des Lilas," Johnny Mercer said he would pen the English lyrics. It became "Once Upon a Summertime" and was one of Blossom's—and Michel's—most popular songs.

Jack Paar was a fan of Blossom's and often had her on his popular television show. Around this time she also shared the bill with Miles Davis at the Village Vanguard six times. In what would be her only mainstream outing she recorded an album for Capitol Records, *May I Come In*. It featured friend and jazz trumpeter Jack Sheldon and songs by Antonio Carlos Jobim, Johnny Mercer and others. But, musical tastes were changing and the record didn't make the impact Blossom had hoped for. In the meantime her friend Annie Ross had opened a club in England and encouraged her to come over for concerts.

At this time she traveled frequently between New York and London. She would spend months at a time using London as a base from which she would tour Europe. She appeared on Dudley Moore's television show and in 1966 began what would be ten consecutive seasons at Ronnie Scott's club. It became a church-like atmosphere as Blossom's followers arranged their chairs to face her and nary a sound was heard. Though bewildering to club-owner Scott, this was the beginning of what Blossom wanted at her club gigs, which she increasingly called "concerts." The response to her Ronnie Scott's engagements led to the recording of four albums on Fontana in the United Kingdom. Two live from Ronnie Scott's (*Blossom Time* and *Sweet Blossom Dearie*) and two in the studio (*Soon It's Gonna Rain* and *That's Just the Way I Want to Be*). These recordings represent the first time Blossom would feature songs like "I'm Hip" and some of her own compositions. It was during one of her trips back home that she met with young songwriter Dave Frishberg who presented her with what would become two of her signature songs, "Peel Me a Grape" and "I'm Hip" (co-written with Bob Dorough), and they remain big favorites.

Around this same time back in London, Blossom was at a friend's house when Georgie Fame's "Yeah Yeah" came on the radio. (Fame is a British singer/guitarist/rock composer.) Blossom had seen Georgie Fame perform and liked him, and upon seeing her friend's children dance around to the record she wrote a melody for him. Her friend suggested they visit her sister, Sandra Harris, who was good at writing lyrics and the result was "Sweet Georgie Fame" and Blossom's songwriting career was launched. She started her own publishing company, Blossom Dearie Music (**blossomdeariemusicpublishing.com**), and special songs, written by her in collaboration with sensitive lyricists, continued to be created up until the early 2000s. In recent years, songs written and published by Blossom have been recorded by Kiri Te Kanawa, Carmen McRae, Maureen McGovern, Tierney Sutton, Yo Yo Ma, and Renee Fleming among others.

While on the David Frost Show in London, Blossom met John Lennon and was delighted to find that he was a fan. When he performed on the show he sang in his higher register and called it his "Blossom Dearie voice." Another tribute song followed, "Hey John," written with Jim Council. Returning to New York, Blossom and Mahriah Blackwolf wrote three of her most endearing numbers, "I Like You, You're Nice," "Touch the Hand of Love," and "Inside a Silent Tear."

Johnny Mercer and Blossom had spent a lot of time together, becoming close friends, and in the early '70s they finally sat down and wrote a song together, "I'm Shadowing You." However, Blossom felt that no one wanted to record her kind of music so she set out to create a master recording herself. Her intention was to shop it around to other record labels and if no one was interested she would keep it for herself. In 1974 she decided to circumvent the label process and, with fan requests and her brother Walter's help, Daffodil Records was established. Further recordings were lovingly crafted from 1975–2000, and Daffodil has the special distinction of being one of the first successful private record labels.

Also in 1974, Blossom's "concerts" resumed (initiated at Ronnie Scott's) and they would continue until her retirement in 2006. Still playing in the same clubs, Blossom also added larger halls and venues to her tours. She began performing more for her specialized audience that had come for one reason: to hear her sing and play. And she kept refining the criteria of her "concerts." This meant no taped music played before shows or between sets, no waitresses or food service while she performed, and no smoking, ever! If venue owners didn't adhere to "The Blossom Dearie Agreement," which also had commentary on crying children and cash registers, she would go home. Blossom's intimate concerts took on a much slower pace than the fast-moving world surrounding them. They were called havens by some, but woe to the person who talked while she sang, or, in later years, didn't turn off their cell phones. Blossom cared deeply about what she gave her fans, and was always there after the show with her Daffodil albums for sale and with time to chat and for photos.

Blossom often recorded as she traveled. Daffodil's first recording, *Blossom Dearie Sings* (1973), was recorded in a midtown London basement. Daffodil's second album, *Blossom Dearie 1975: From the Meticulous to the Sublime,* was recorded in Los Angeles. The title was suggested by a writer for *The New Yorker*, Rogers Whittaker, who had also named her record label. Volume 3, entitled *My New Celebrity Is You,* was recorded in New York. The title track was Johnny Mercer's final composition, a gift to Blossom. Volume 4, *Winchester in Apple Blossom Time,* was recorded in San Francisco and became the official song of the Apple Blossom Festival's 50th Anniversary in 1977. Volume 5, *Needlepoint Magic,* brought Blossom back to New York City, in concert at Reno Sweeney's club.

The first five Daffodil recordings were expressions of Blossom's nature as a musician. From electric piano with a pop sensibility to solo acoustic piano creating an intimate mood, to live performance as she guided her audiences through the sometimes low, sometimes funny life of love. The 1980s saw more of this expression and experimentation and delivery of her audience's favorite songs.

Blossom's collaborators were often her longtime friends. Mike Renzi delivered topnotch jazz arrangements and what Blossom called "mentoring" on her recordings in the '80s and early '90s. Her friend Bob Dorough did two more duets with her on the recording entitled *Simply*. Other friends, including Phil Woods and Grady Tate, sat in on her 1982 jazz album *Positively*. In 1984 Blossom's friend, songwriter John Wallowitch, provided her with the comedy song "Bruce," a song about a very confused drag queen lacking in the most basic sense of style. Her "funny songs" as she called them increasingly became a staple in her concerts. Dave Frishberg added to her repertoire with "My Attorney Bernie," which Blossom sang at the White House in 1993 in tribute to all the Washington lawyers in attendance.

The recording *Songs of Chelsea* returned Blossom to her intimate combo with a record featuring popular songs from her annual runs at the Ballroom in Chelsea, New York City. Blossom's concert series there were annual affairs because of her popularity and peculiarity. Preferring to be in bed by the eleven o'clock news, Blossom began her concerts at 6:30 in the evening. Her audiences were made up of early partiers and post-workday folks. The age range was as large as the enthusiasm of the crowd. Blossom, along with Bob Dorough, had composed for and performed on ABC's "Schoolhouse Rock," and that viewership had grown up and found her once again. After a good show and good time she walked home alone.

Two CD releases in 1991 saw some of Blossom's most beautiful work. *Tweedledum & Tweedledee* included Blossom Dearie and Jack Segal songs "I Don't Remember," "I Thought I Heard a Hummingbird," and "Love Is on the Way." The album was a blend of acoustic piano, synthesizer, sensitive percussion and a mood and feeling only Blossom could create. *Christmas Spice So Very Nice* is a Christmas album for couples. Songs of love and excitement replace the usual standards that recording artists often choose. Her brother Walter W. Birchett composed the song "Christmas" with her. John Wallowitch returned with a song entitled, "Liz, Ralph, and Calvin"—you guessed it, an homage to the famous clothing designers. Many years later Blossom said it was only Claiborne who sent clothes.

After these recordings were made, Blossom continued her world travels to receptive audiences from Iceland to Australia, London to Hong Kong. She finally landed back in New York City around 1998. Although she still traveled, it was much less frequently. She had found a nest, as it were, in Danny's Skylight Room, a small cabaret/restaurant on Restaurant Row near Broadway. Each concert was a survey of Blossom's "hits" and each weekend the faithful made their pilgrimage to see her, often times with standing room only.

Blossom had a health scare in 2000 and had become a little more frail. That year she released what would be her final recording, *Blossom's Planet*. The same words that had always been used to describe her work were once again rolled out. "Delicate," "sophisticated," "beautiful," and "definitive" were applied to her recordings of "Love Dance" and Jobim's "Wave." Another outstanding track from her live shows was Stephen Sondheim's "The Ladies Who Lunch." Blossom continued to perform in New York City most weekends through 2007 when illness forced her into retirement. She remained at her Greenwich Village apartment where she died peacefully on February 9, 2009. Blossom's older brother Barney had managed Daffodil Records for many years and continues to do so to this day. The future of her label rests in restoring and releasing the complete back catalog through Blossom's website, **www.blossomdearie.com**.

© Jaime Smith, 2011
Edited by Sharon Grace Powers

BRING ALL YOUR LOVE ALONG

Words by JACK SEGAL
Music by BLOSSOM DEARIE

Pop Ballad

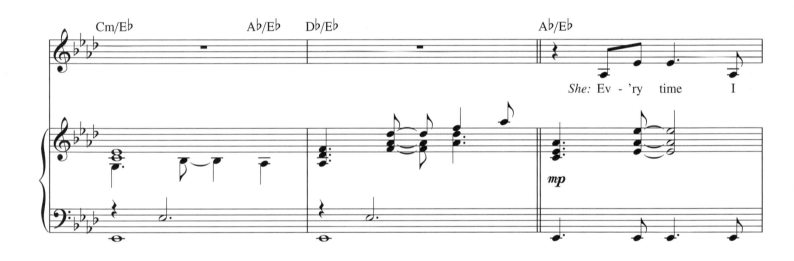

She: Ev - 'ry time I

miss you, _____ my phone is sure to ring.

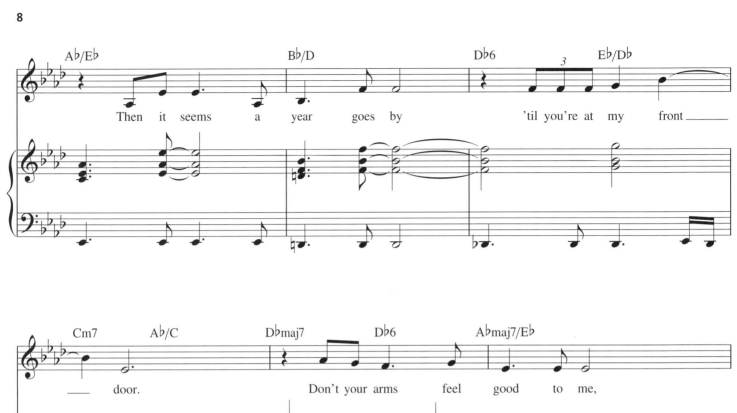

Then it seems a year goes by 'til you're at my front ___

___ door. Don't your arms feel good to me,

so warm and safe and strong. Ev-'ry time you

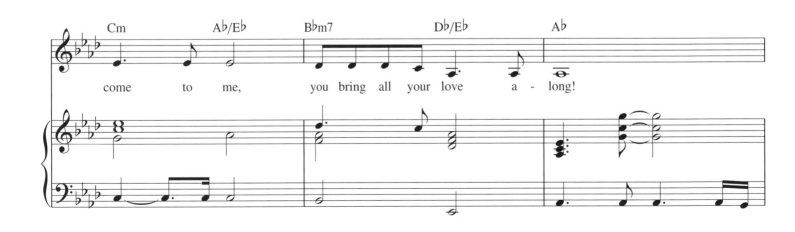

come to me, you bring all your love a - long!

song. "Hur - ry home," you sing to me,

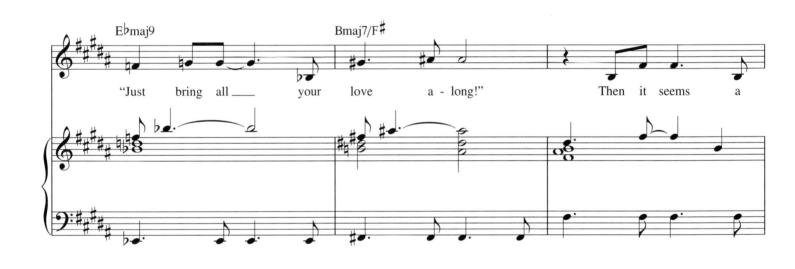

"Just bring all ___ your love a - long!" Then it seems a

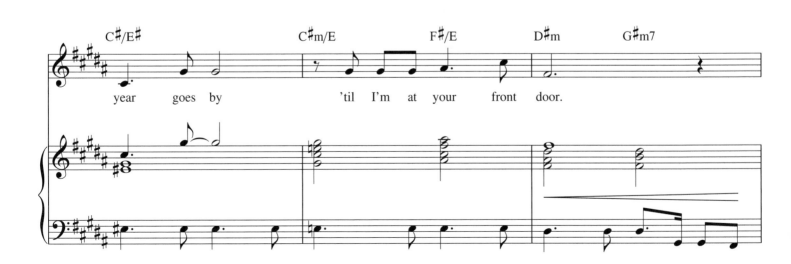

year goes by 'til I'm at your front door.

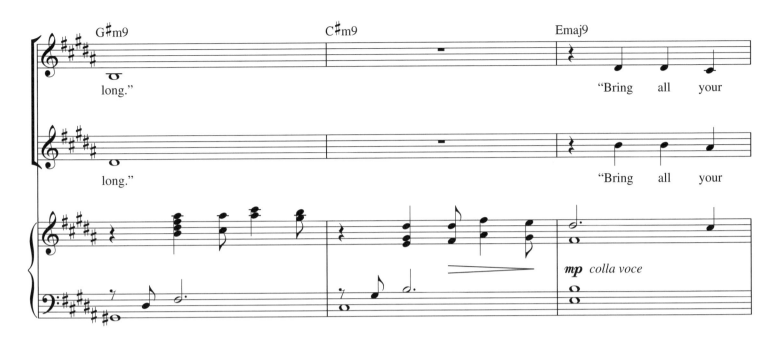

BYE-BYE COUNTRY BOY

Words by JACK SEGAL
Music by BLOSSOM DEARIE

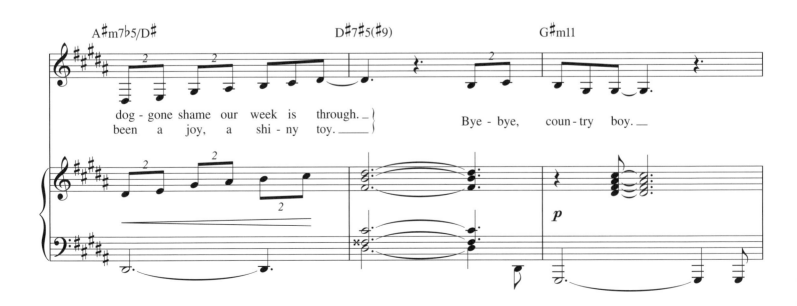

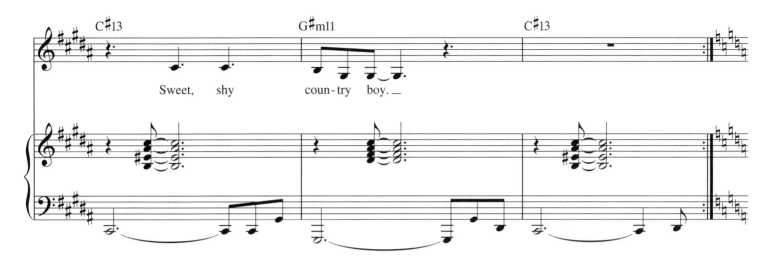

Sweet, shy coun-try boy. __

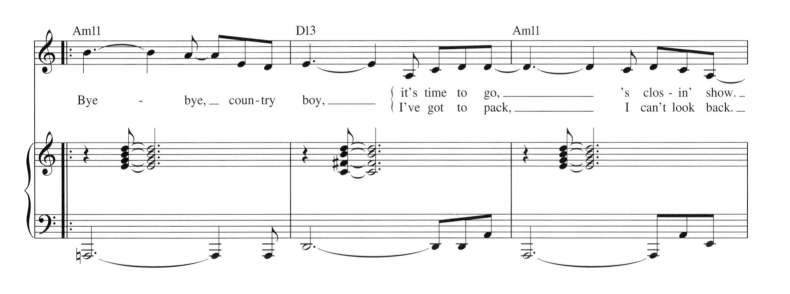

Bye - bye, __ coun-try boy, _____ { it's time to go, _____ 's clos-in' show. __
I've got to pack, _____ I can't look back. __

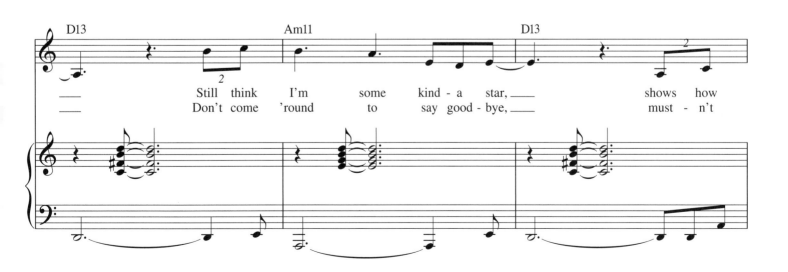

__ Still think I'm some kind-a star, __ shows how
__ Don't come 'round to say good-bye, __ must-n't

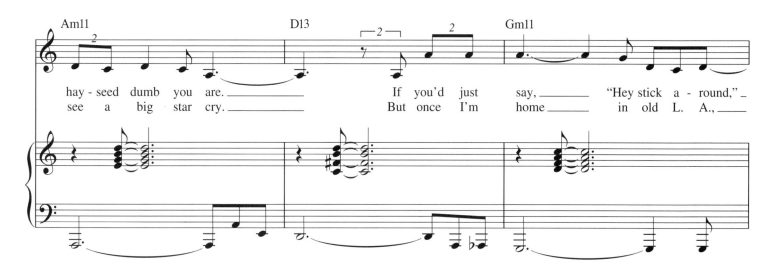

hay - seed dumb you are._____ If you'd just say,_____ "Hey stick a - round,"_
see a big star cry. But once I'm home_____ in old L. A.,_

I'd tell my group,_____ "I ain't leav - in' town!"_
my heart and mind_____ will be miles a - way_____

But
still

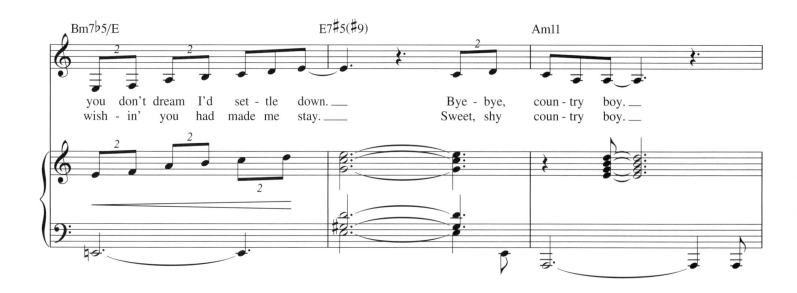

you don't dream I'd set - tle down._____ Bye - bye, coun - try boy._
wish - in' you had made me stay._____ Sweet, shy coun - try boy._

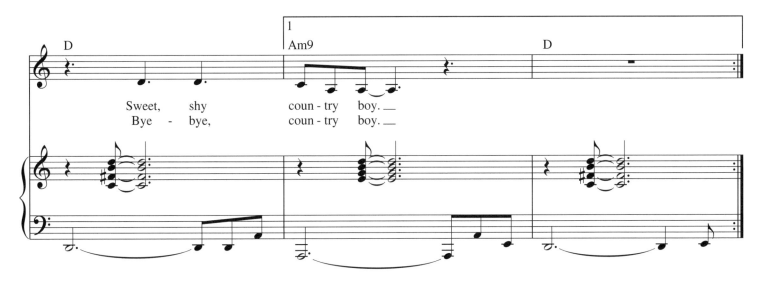

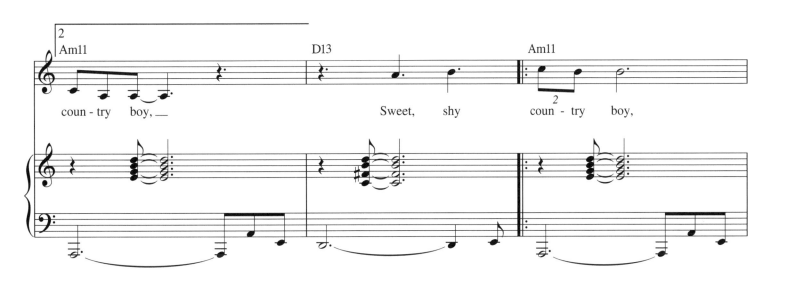

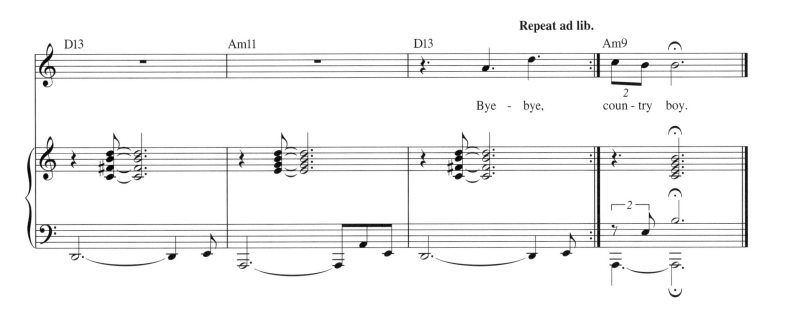

'DEED I DO

Words and Music by WALTER HIRSCH
and FRED ROSE

20

I LIKE YOU, YOU'RE NICE

Words by MAHRIAH BLACKWOLF
Music by BLOSSOM DEARIE

INSIDE A SILENT TEAR

Words by MAHRIAH BLACKWOLF
Music by BLOSSOM DEARIE

Slow, tender Bossa (♩ = 92)

In - side a Si - lent Tear___ I have a si - lent dream,___
laugh too much___ to hide the emp - ti - ness,___
find - ing love___ when it's not meant to be,___

That some - times sails a - cross___ the pat - terns of my
To lose the lone - li - ness,___ I'm not the laugh - ing
What is re - al - i - ty?___ And can it be de -

I WON'T DANCE

Words and Music by JIMMY McHUGH, DOROTHY FIELDS,
JEROME KERN, OSCAR HAMMERSTEIN II
and OTTO HARBACH

I'M SHADOWING YOU

Words by JOHNNY MERCER
Music by BLOSSOM DEARIE

Ev - 'ry-where you go, I think____ you ought to know, I'm Shad - ow - ing You,____
Like I said be - fore, I'm camp - in' at your door, I'm Shad - ow - ing You,____

Turn a - round 'n' find, I'm half____ a step be - hind, I'm
How can you es - cape? I'm get - tin' out a tape and

IT MIGHT AS WELL BE SPRING
from STATE FAIR

Lyrics by OSCAR HAMMERSTEIN II
Music by RICHARD RODGERS

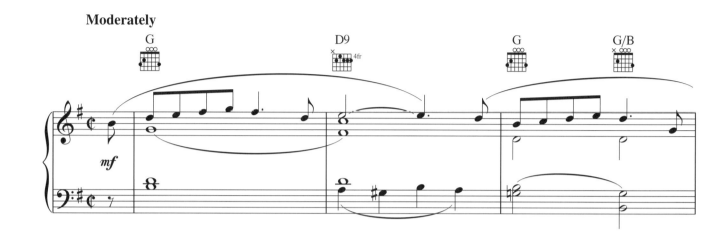

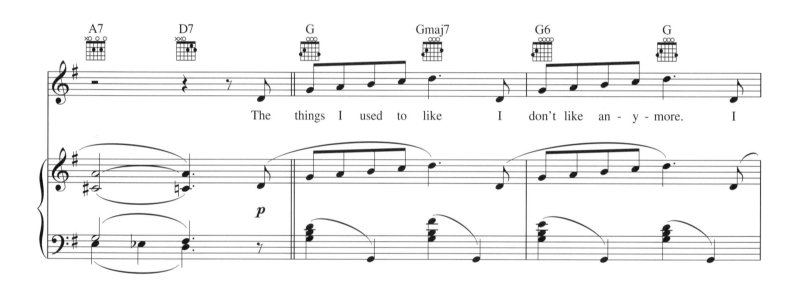

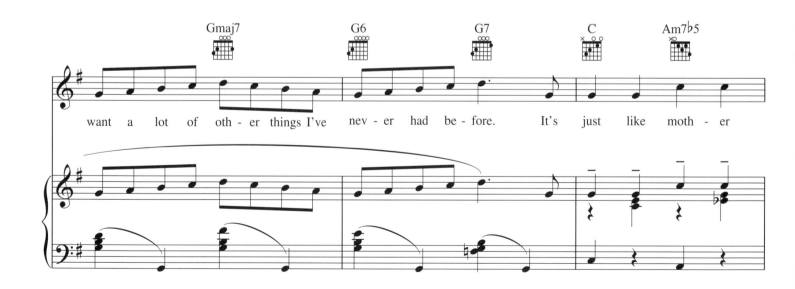

LONG DADDY GREEN

Words by DAVE FRISHBERG
Music by BLOSSOM DEARIE

Sweet are the pleas-ures that mon-ey can-not buy. But they're

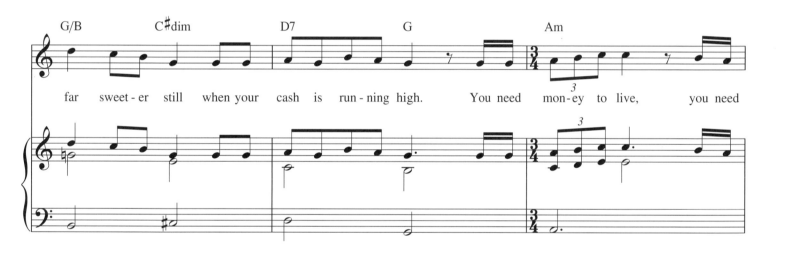

far sweet-er still when your cash is run-ning high. You need mon-ey to live, you need

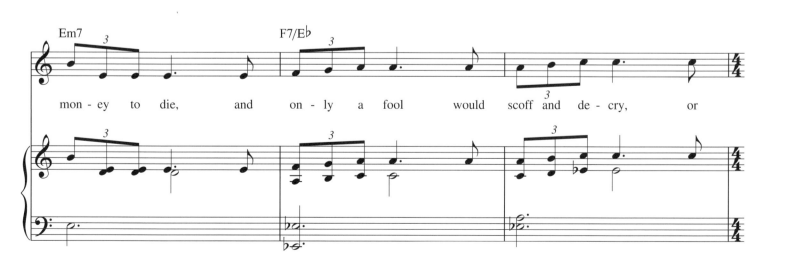

mon-ey to die, and on-ly a fool would scoff and de-cry, or

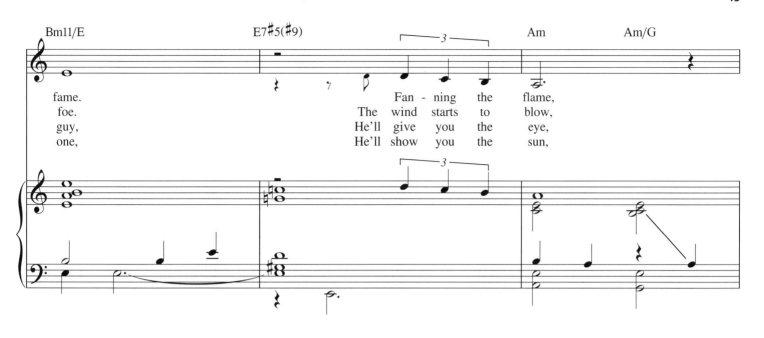

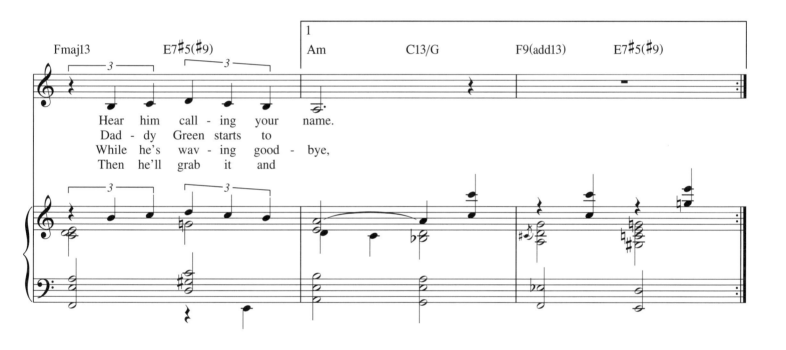

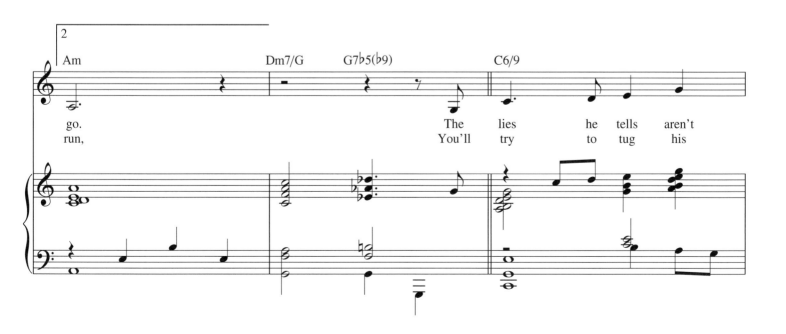

(There Ought to Be A)
MOONLIGHT SAVING TIME

Words and Music by IRVING KAHAL
and HARRY RICHMAN

ONCE UPON A SUMMERTIME

English Lyric by JOHNNY MERCER
Original Lyric by EDDIE MARNAY
Music by EDDIE BARCLAY and MICHEL LEGRAND

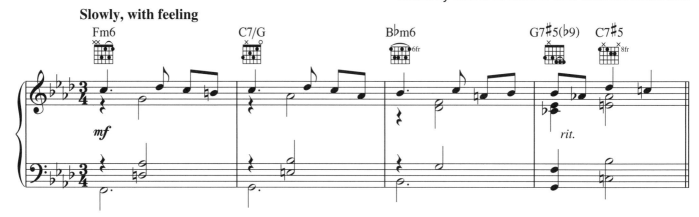

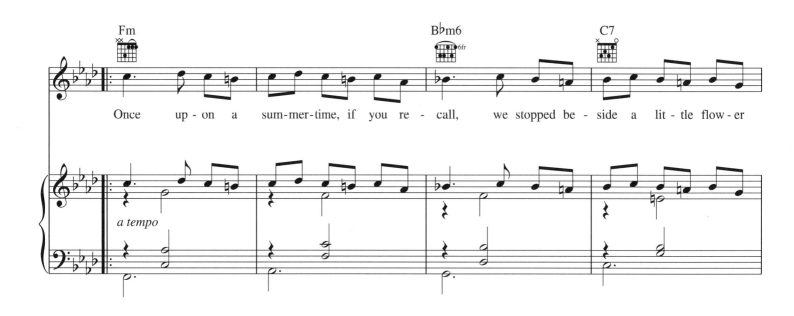

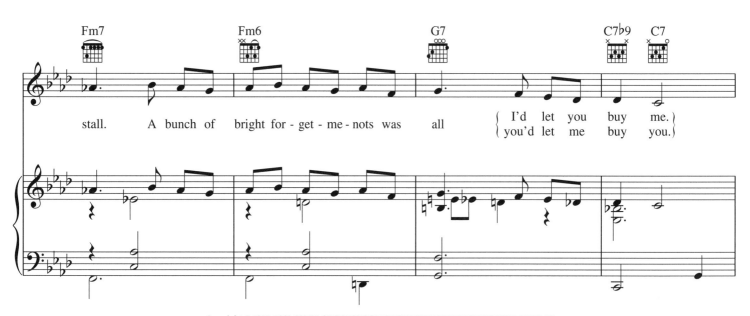

TOUCH THE HAND OF LOVE

Words by MAHRIAH BLACKWOLF
Music by BLOSSOM DEARIE

PEEL ME A GRAPE

Words and Music by
DAVE FRISHBERG
Arrangement by BLOSSOM DEARIE

60

SWEET GEORGIE FAME

Words and Music by BLOSSOM DEARIE
and SANDRA HARRIS

Moderate Jazz Waltz (♩ = 100)
D6/9
C♯m7(11)
F♯7-9 -5 -13
Bm7
Words and music are all that I need,
heard him one night quite by chance,
Am9
D13
Gmaj7
G6/9
C♯13(+9)
F♯13
(-13)
I will fol - low where ev - er they lead,
Now where ev - er I'm walk - in' I dance,

WINCHESTER IN APPLE BLOSSOM TIME

Words by WALTER W. BIRCHETT
Music by BLOSSOM DEARIE

Gentle Waltz

Scoo-bie-doo (etc.)

In spring I find a fra-grance fair _____ when

ap-ple blos-soms fill the air. The birds, the flow'rs, the white-tailed

Guitar Symbols by Gene Bertoncini